ISM Working Paper No. 18

Simon Stotz, Ralf A. Brickau, Christoph Moss,
Daniel Meierhof

Measuring and Restoring customer trust - an explorative research based on the VW Diesel gate scandal

Stotz, Simon; Brickau, Ralf A.; Moss, Christoph, Meierhof, Daniel: Measuring and Restoring customer trust - an explorative research based on the VW Diesel gate scandal

Herstellung und Verlag: BoD – Books on Demand, Norderstedt
ISBN 978-3-7557-2429-2

ISM - International School of Management gGmbH
Otto-Hahn-Str. 19 · 44227 Dortmund
www.ism.de
Tel.: 0231.975139-0 · Fax: 0231.975139-39
ism.dortmund@ism.de

Stotz, Simon; Brickau, Ralf A.; Moss, Christoph; Meierhof, Daniel: Measuring and Restoring customer trust - an explorative research based on the VW Diesel gate scandal. Dortmund und NoderstedtMünster, BoD, 2021 (Working Paper 18)
ISBN 978-3-7557-2429-2

Contents

List of Figures

Abstract

Much has been written about trust. Despite the fact that there is a general understanding of how important trust is in interpersonal and business relations it becomes obvious that this construct remains somewhat indistinct when it comes to pinning down how trust is build or destroyed, how levels of trust can be measured precisely and how trust can be restored if it has deteriorated.

Therefor this research makes use of an earlier model by Kreikenberg (2013) which provides one of the most comprehensive models for measuring trust via seven trust-building factors in five trust-dimensions. This model, due to its complexity, has been adapted and simplified. Moreover, the model was enhanced to include an empirical approach to detect trust building measures to restore trust.

The adapted model was put to an empirical test on the Volkswagen Diesel Exhaust Scandal of 2015 with VW-customers. Findings show that the adapted model could provide results on which dimensions and factors show a deterioration of trust and simultaneously how trust gaps detected could be filled via measures proposed by customers.

Although this research must be called explorative, results give some indication that the new model appears to work satisfactory and should be put to further empirical tests in other companies and Industry to find further proof for a general applicability.

1   Introduction

In September 2015, it became known for the first time in the USA that the Volkswagen Group had been using manipulation software for several years to change the exhaust gas values in diesel vehicles in order to comply with the specifications for exhaust gas values in test mode. Under real conditions, however, these values were significantly higher (cf. Schmidt 2016). These inspections uncovered the Volkswagen diesel exhaust scandal. On the one hand, the Group had to spend just under 26 billion euros between 2015 and 2017 due to manipulating the exhaust emission values (cf. Volkswagen 2012 after Bratzel 2018), and on the other hand, a loss of image, overtime for managers and changes in the personnel policy of senior executives led to further indirect costs (cf. Bratzel 2018). In addition, the company was fined one billion Euro by the Braunschweig public prosecutor's office in 2018, which increased the costs incurred by DES for VW to around 27 billion Euro (cf. Bratzel 2018).

The uncovered DES not only decimated public and political confidence in VW as the largest representative of the German automotive industry, but also the credibility of the entire industry. Furthermore, VW was not transparent in its handling of the accusations surrounding the diesel emissions scandal, resulting in new incriminating findings and investigations with corresponding results were repeatedly made over long periods in the course of the investigations (cf. Bratzel 2018). Research confirms a loss of the public's confidence and credibility of the automotive industry. A study from January 2018 confirmed the loss of trust in the German automotive industry in absolute numbers. According to the study, trust has fallen from 61% in 2015 (before publication of the exhaust emissions scandal) to 35% (Edelman 2018 after Bratzel 2018).Although, the concept of trust is defined and explained later in this paper, there are no known concepts for developing measures to rebuild trust destroyed in business relationships such as between VW and customers affected by the emissions scandal. Kreikenberg developed a concept for measuring customer trust, on which this research is based. According to him there are five decisive dimensions of trust, which represent those elements where people can perceive trust in companies (cf. Kreikenberg 2013).

Furthermore, seven trust-building factors can be assigned to each dimension and have to be examined. These factors are able to build and strengthen trust within those dimensions (cf. Kreikenberg 2013). Analysing the perception of these factors within the five dimensions can detect where factors underperform and consequently a loss of trust can be identified. However, the model does not offer the possibility to create measures with which companies are able to resolve trust gaps uncovered.

This research will build on the model developed by Kreikenberg (2013). As mentioned before, there are no possibilities to simultaneously identify and fill trust gaps within this model. Thus, a significant research gap has clearly been identified, which needs to be closed with the use of the measures applied in this paper. Therefor the research aim is a) to identify those gaps and b) establish measures to provide decisive actions for VW to regain trust within its customer base, i.e. fill the gaps identified. After all, a stable basis of trust between customer and company is essential for an ongoing functional relationship (cf. Rossmann 2010). Due to this it is of high importance to investigate whether and how the described trust problems can be solved.

2   Theoretical research

The following explanations on the subject of trust are intended to give a brief but comprehensive impression of what trust basically is and how it can be lost. This will help to better understand the research that follows.

2.1   Trust

According to Peters (2008), trust is defined as follows: Trust is the voluntary provision of a high-risk advance without intentional controls by forming the experience-based expectation that the trusted party will not voluntarily act to the detriment of the trusting party, or at least not tend to behave reciprocally in an uncertain future (cf. Peters

2008). The vulnerability of a trusting party is the tool with which he/she creates a relationship based on trust (cf. Luhmann 2000 after Hatak 2018).

The term trust is understood as a positive expectation on the part of one side regarding the behaviour of the other (cf. Lewicki et al. 1998 after Bagdoniene/Jakstaite 2009). These expectations should always be linked to beneficial behavioural outcomes (cf. Suh et al. 2006 after Bagdoniene/Jakstaite 2009). The development of trust is promoted when one side is willing to invest something of importance in the achievement of a goal and believes in the competence, knowledge and intentions of another side and assumes reliability, resulting in a stronger bond between the parties (cf. Cowles 1996 after Bagdoniene/Jakstaite 2009).

Trust is based on a relationship. The decisive factor is the relationship between a person who offers trust (e.g. VW customer) and a person/party who accepts the trust (e.g. VW). The expectations of the behaviour of the trusted party play a decisive role. Within the framework of this relationship there is a risk that the party to whom the trust was offered will abuse it. Other important factors are the length of the relationship between the two parties and the reciprocity. This is referred to as social trust (cf. Balderjahn 2010).

2.2   Loss of trust

The first incident that can result in a loss of trust is that of making mistakes. However, it can be stated that marginal mistakes do not directly result in a loss of trust. When mistakes occur more frequently, then trust is threatened for the reason of two following aspects (cf. Davies/Olmedo-Cifuentes 2016): The reliability of the company is seen as inadequate, which may be an indication of a deficit in competence but is a significant factor in terms of trust (cf. Zhong et al. 2014; Johnson-George & Swap 1982 after Davies/Olmedo-Cifuentes 2016). In addition, it is emphasised that such behaviour is not predictable and the company is not credible (cf. Mayer et al. 1995 after Davies/Olmedo-Cifuentes 2016).

The next aspect deals with being untruthful. The fundamental principle of any trustful cooperation is to tell the truth on the part of the trust-taker and being honest is often seen as a sign of trust (cf. Larzelere and Huston 1980; Johnson-George and Swap 1982 after Davies/Olmedo-Cifuentes 2016). If the party is trusted but behaves contrary to expectations, this can lead to a loss of trust and if this behaviour is supplemented by deception, trust can suffer irreparable damage (cf. Schweitzer et al. 2006 after Davies/Olmedo-Cifuentes 2016). Thus, it can be said that enterprises run the risk of losing trust if they are not honest (cf. Davies/Olmedo-Cifuentes 2016). According to the information obtained, if, for example, a large automotive group such as VW issues false news and advertising messages and knowingly tries to deceive customers, there is a great risk of a sustained loss of trust. This form of entrepreneurial misconduct therefore represents a particularly pronounced danger, because, as explained in previous sections, trust is an important basis for customer retention and thus competitive advantage.

Probably the most negative behaviour of a company, which can result in the loss of trust, is disregarding laws. Compliance with laws is seen as the fundamental virtue of a company, as it is assumed that there is no willingness to risk legality due to unlawful business activities (cf. Davies/Olmedo-Cifuentes 2016). Even if no laws are broken, companies can profit from certain loopholes or grey areas in the law, such as the so-called 'tax-aggressive policy'. Here, entrepreneurial activities are carried out in such a way that corporate income tax can be paid via places with a less tax burden. Since this behaviour is not considered to be morally sound (cf. Lanis and Richardson 2012 after Davies/Olmedo-Cifuentes 2016), the outcome will probably not only have a negative effect on the trust factor but will also have a negative influence on corporate integrity, which is fundamental to trust (cf. Morgan and Hunt 1994 after Davies/Olmedo-Cifuentes 2016).

2.3   Five trust building dimensions

Dimension (1) *company trust*: *Company trust* "is the belief that the company will fulfil all its obligations as understood by the buyer" (Comer et al. 1999: 62). From the behaviour and operations of a company, the perception of the degree of trustworthiness on the part of customers will lead to customer trust in a company (cf. Shockley-Zalabak/Morreale 2011).

The prevailing opinion in the literature is that the implementation of trustworthy principles in the organisation is a prerequisite for customer trust (cf. Shockley-Zalabak/Morreale 2011). As a result, it must be emphasised that the stringent implementation of corporate governance has a significant impact on the trustworthiness of the organization (cf. Ennew/Sekhon 2007). It also must be noted that good image and corporate reputation can have a positive effect on promoting customer trust. Good will and competence are further parameters that are perceived by the customer and can establish trust. Ethical behaviour of an organisation promotes trust, unethical behaviour undermines trust (cf. Leonidou et al. 2013). If the customer observes unethical behaviour on the part of the company, this can have a negative impact on the trust placed in the company by the customer (cf. Leonidou et al. 2013).

Dimension (2) *salesperson trust*: Literature expresses that trust in an organisation is based on trust between two people. The dimension of this multidimensional relationship level is trust in the salesperson (cf. Fulmer/Gelfand 2012; Comer et al. 1999). Customer trust and thus customer behaviour is decisively influenced by the behaviour of the salesperson and the first impression he/she makes (cf. Wünschmann/Müller

2006). Uncertainties of the customer are minimized by a stable trust in the salesperson. Similarly, trust in the salesperson increases trust in the brand and/or the product (cf. Guenzi et al. 2009).

Dimension (3) *product trust*: There are different ways for trust to arise at the customer level, e.g. when it comes to a product or service. A distinction must be made between trust in goods and trust in services. A product has haptic qualities for the customer as opposed to a service. For a customer relationship to continue, the customer expectation in the goods or services must be fulfilled (cf. Comer et al. 1999). Further literature emphasises that the degree of trust between service provider and customer determines the appreciation of the relationship. Thus, trust acts as an important element in maintaining such a relationship (cf. Doney & Cannon 1997; Sharma & Pattersson 1999 after Bagdoniene/Jakstaite 2009) and in realising the potential for success (cf. Kramer & Tyler 1995 after Bagdoniene/Jakstaite 2009). This fact highlights the relevance of a stable interpersonal level, especially in the service sector.

Dimension (4) *product brand trust*: The signal effect of a well-known brand reduces the information asymmetry between company and customer subjectively perceived by the customer and thus creates a basis of trust and lowers the risk of selection by the customer when choosing a company (cf. Martín/Camarero 2005). Additional literature supports this definition of brand trust. It is stressed that brand trust is the degree to which a consumer can rely on a brand. Furthermore, strong brand trust reduces perceived purchase risks (cf. Esch 2004 after Ahlström/Gesper 2007).

Dimension (5) *value-added-services*: Value-added-services (VAS) which the customer recognizes as an advantage can additionally support trust and strengthen customer loyalty. VAS can enhance the core product and increase the perception of value and benefit (cf. Berndt et al. 2010; Jänig 2004). In addition to customer loyalty, they are also suitable for inducing repeat purchases and for word-of-mouth advertising to friends and acquaintances (cf. Berndt et al. 2010). This definition is supported by other authors. Additional literature emphasises that VAS result in a better customer orientation perceived by the customer. Furthermore, VAS ensure increasing customer satisfaction and loyalty, which ultimately guarantees long-term business success (cf. Homburg/Garbe 1996; Stauss 1998 after Bruhn/Straßer 2014)

2.4   Seven trust building factors

Factor (1) *Competence:* The term competence, a synonym for ability, implies that tasks are mastered in a result-oriented manner using professional knowledge and skills (cf. Colquitt et al. 2007). In addition to knowledge and abilities, the term competence also includes universal knowledge and social competence in interpersonal interaction (Gabarro, 1978, after Colquitt et al. 2007). Trust is not only created by affection and goodwill but also in partnerships on a business level in particular, requiring specialist knowledge and expertise (cf. Pirson 2007).

Factor (2) *Benevolence*: The manner, in which one person meets the interests of another, is referred to as benevolence. A prerequisite for this is selfless behaviour, which is determined by the care and support of the related parties (cf. Colquitt et al. 2007; Pirson 2007). Even spontaneous aspects of interpersonal relationships are encouraged by benevolent behaviour between two parties (cf. Lorbeer 2003; Mayer et al. 1995).

Factor (3) *Integrity*: Integrity is "defined as the extent to which a trustee is believed to adhere to sound moral and ethical principles (...)" (Colquitt et al. 2007: 910). From this, it can be deduced that such persons have a close connection to certain values and thus support and personally represent them. Integrity refers to conduct that complies with moral and ethical standards. Integrity thus excludes disregarding ethical principles to achieve objectives (cf. Lorbeer 2003). The result of behaving with integrity is that others are given the opportunity to forecast one´s behaviour – i.e. that of the integrity party – (Lind 2001 after Colquitt et al. 2007).

Factor (4) *Reliability*: Also independent of moral and ethical aspects, reliability improves the predictability of behaviour. Future behaviour can be predicted, which can result in an increase in trust (cf. Pirson 2007). However, this only succeeds under the condition that a person behaves consistently, which results in a gain in certainty (Ring 1996 after Lorbeer 2003).

Factor (5) *Transparency*: The term transparency implies that all circumstances are openly and comprehensively explained (cf. Mohr/Nevin 1990), which is particularly important in the case of an asymmetry of knowledge (cf. Lewis 2007). This reduces the subjective perception of risk and improves the flow of information (cf. Mohr/Nevin 1990; Schoorman et al. 2007).

Factor (6) *Identification*: Kreikenberg says that "Identification with, as well as sympathy for, another person can be described as affective element among the trust antecedents. Sympathy therefore goes beyond the perceived competence of another person" (Kreikenberg 2013: 62). Trust is grounded on the idea that the intentions and motives of people with sympathy are of a rather positive nature (cf. Nicholson et al. 2001 after Lorbeer 2003).

Factor (7) *Reputation*: "Reputation is defined as a third-party evaluation" (Ganesan 1994; Lorbeer 2003 after Kreikenberg 2013: 63). Particularly in the case of a lack of information at the starting point of a contact, the presentation of third parties is used to make up for the lack of knowledge to make one's own assessment (cf. Pirson 2007). The size of a company and its position in the market are equally important for a good reputation (cf. Lorbeer 2003). After the dimensions and factors have been presented, the following presentation by Kreikenberg (2013) is intended to illustrate the relationship between dimensions and factors regarding customer trust in business interactions and relationships.

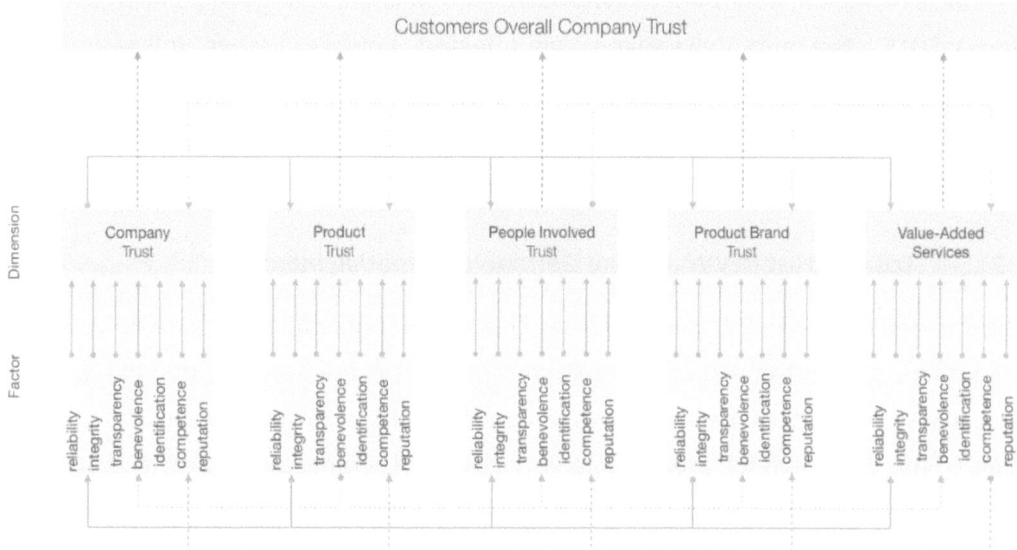

Figure 1:   Trust model for customer trust in companies
Kreikenberg 2013: 96

3   Practical Case VW

The following chapter deals with the most relevant facts about the VW diesel exhaust scandal. In addition to a comprehensive presentation of the scandal, it also deals with the dimensions and factors mentioned above in relation to the scandal.

3.1   VW diesel exhaust scandal

In September 2015, VW confessed to the US Environmental Protection Agency (EPA) that it had installed unauthorised software in diesel vehicles which triggered the shutdown of the exhaust system. As a result, the exhaust gas values of these vehicles were manipulated by engine control software in such a way that cars running in the test environment complied with the legally permitted exhaust gas values for NOx (cf. Bratzel 2018).

Various US American institutions carried out tests with VW diesel vehicles in a test environment and on the road. The results showed enormous differences in NOx emission values, which finally exposed VW by the US authorities. VW explained this with a software error and recalled about 500,000 vehicles, promising to rectify this error. The authority 'California Air Resources Board' (CARB), however, could not find any improvement in the emission values and threatened not to approve any of VW's models to go to market in 2016, whereupon the company admitted the fraud on September

3rd, 2015 (cf. Bratzel 2018). As a result, the American government ordered VW to buy back nearly 500,000 two-litres diesel engine vehicles from affected American customers of the 2009-2015 series (cf. Yates, Sally after Netflix 2018: 3 min.). The total number of vehicles affected, determined towards the end of 2015, was eleven million (cf. Eckl-Dorna 2015). Not only Volkswagen was affected, however, other Volkswagen AG brands were also involved in the DES. Several models of Audi, Seat and Skoda were affected as well. Other manufacturers such as BMW, Ford and Mercedes Benz were also involved in the emissions affair (cf. Andresen 2019).

3.2   Loss of trust in VW and the German automotive industry

The damage caused to VW is more far-reaching than simple financial expenditure. It is the loss of trust on the part of the customers as well as the deterioration of VW´s image. VW's current CEO, Herbert Diess, emphasises the enormous loss of trust, especially in the VW brand (cf. Menzel 2019). A statistical survey, conducted in 2016, confirms that many of the respondents have a less positive opinion about VW after the DES became known. In Figure 2 the participants' opinion about VW after the DES is illustrated.

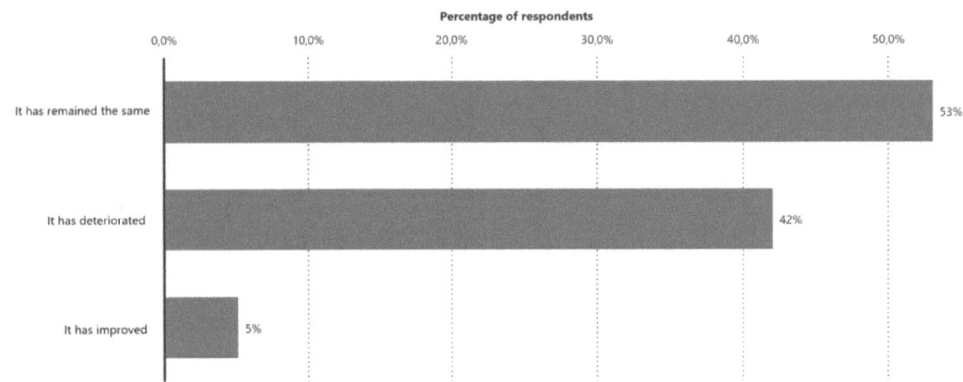

Figure 2:   **Opinion of the (German) population on VW after the diesel scandal in Germany 2016**
Translated from Statista 2016

Due to the lack of more recent surveys a comparison to the change in peoples' opinion about VW over the years cannot be made.

In the 2016 issue of Volkswagen's sustainability magazine, it is emphasised that although the penalties are immense, the damage to reputation is greater. The decisive factor in improving customer relations is much more in focus on the part of the company and less the compliance with legal requirements (cf. Gietl 2016). The following figure outlines the internationally conducted reputation study of 'Global RepTrak 100', in which VW had to cope with a massive deterioration from 2015 to 2016. Trust is also a key factor in the study. As the overall rating of VW has fallen, the factor trust has also deteriorated as a result. This demonstrates the enormous intangible and immaterial loss of the company.

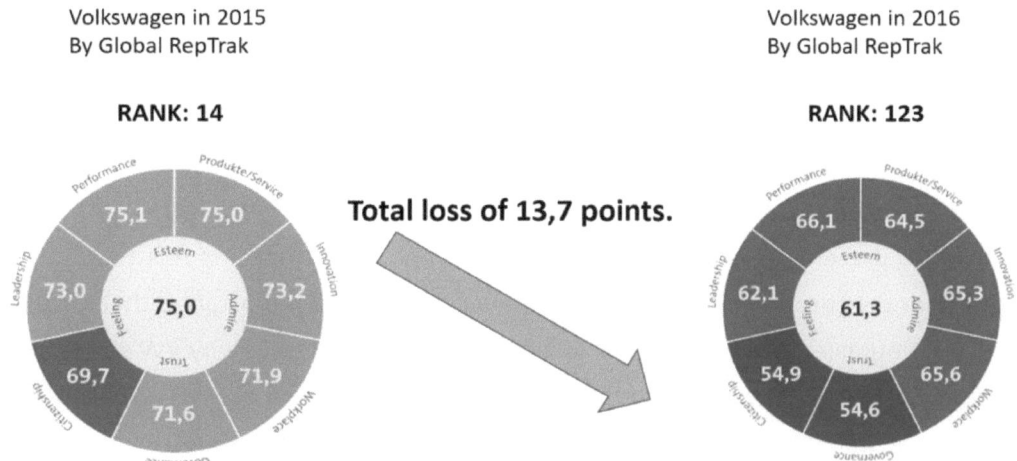

Figure 3:   **Global loss of reputation of Volkswagen from 2015 to 2016**
Own presentation, based on Richter 2016: 19

3.3   Five dimensions and seven factors that build trust

Regarding the VW DES, this section will make clear in which dimensions and in which factors there might be trust gaps. If a concrete identification of the trust gaps regarding the corresponding dimensions and factors, according to Kreikenberg (2013), is not possible, there is reason to investigate these trust gaps. Hence it is essential to highlight which dimensions and factors might have suffered from the VW DES.

As was made clear in the previous sections, the VW DES had various far-reaching consequences. It became clear that the trust of customers and the public has fundamentally suffered because of the DES. It is striking, however, that VW is still the world's leading car manufacturer in terms of sales in 2019 and, as shown in Figure 4, is posting steadily growing sales figures despite DES in 2015.

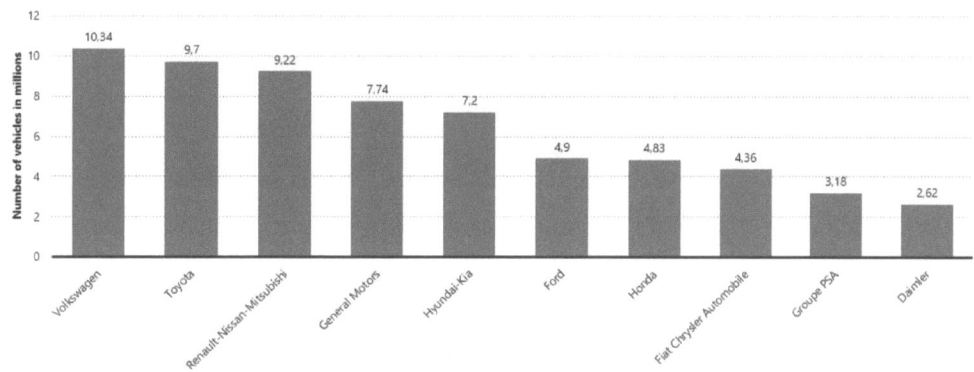

Figure 4:   **Global biggest car manufacturers by vehicle sales in 2019**
Translated from Statista 2020

Stotz, Simon; Brickau, Ralf A.; Moss, Christoph; Meierhof, Daniel:
Measuring and Restoring customer trust - an explorative research based on the VW Diesel
gate scandal

The enormous sales and turnover figures imply that, despite the scandal and despite the extensive loss of trust VW still commands enough confidence and prestige in the eyes of customers to remain world market leader in the industry. However, it cannot be anticipated in how far sales would have been different without the DES. Additionally, it is of interest whether a deterioration of trust may have occurred in other dimensions than the product itself which at a first view has not suffered substantially.

As stated before, it is important to have confidence in a company, a brand, or a seller in order to preserve trust over time. It can be emphasised that it is relatively unimportant for the consumer how a product is functioning, more important is that it works at all (cf. Neumaier 2010). This point of view could be the reason, why VW still retains a strong market power. Although the actual trust of customers has been shaken, the vehicles are still of high quality and function well. The way it functions is insignificant at this point, because according to Neumaier (2010), the customer simply wants to be able to rely on it working. Food scandals, for example, are also quickly forgotten (cf. Neumaier 2010), which is an indication that the fundamental trust in a functioning system is not easily shaken. Nevertheless, it must be emphasised at this point that the entire system, in this case VW, must still be trusted in by customers. When this is no longer the case, the customer may no longer trust in a functioning business process in that company and could turn away as a result.

Figure 3 also illustrates the loss of confidence in some of the measures described in a previous chapter, which clearly shows that there is a need for action. Terms like product trust or trust in general are to be emphasised in this context and damaged the reputation of the company, according to the survey of 'RepTrak' (cf. Richter after Volkswagen AG 2016).

As can be deducted in the present case, there are trust gaps at VW regarding the DES. Even if these do not appear to have considerable effect on the company's success, the damage due to a possible deterioration of trust cannot be quantified clearly. The fact that the trust of customers and the public has been shaken was clearly emphasised in the previous sections. However which of the dimensions and factors defined by Kreikenberg (2013) are affected must be identified within an empirical investigation.

Therefore, general assumptions can be made so far. The trust-building dimensions and factors which were ultimately affected are to be determined, within the framework of empirical part of this paper.

3.4   Derivation of research hypotheses

H1:	a) The five trust-building dimensions are of different relevance to VW customers. b) The seven trust-building factors are of different relevance to VW customers.

H2: Particular constellations between trust-building dimensions and trust-building factors indicate trust gaps within the DES at VW for Customers.

H3: Within the compositional framework of the trust-building dimensions and trust-building factors, VW customers are able to give precise reasons for the loss of trust in the Volkswagen AG.

H4: Identified gaps in trust can be effectively closed via adapted measures that meet the expectations of VW customers.

4 Empirical Investigation

The empirical part deals with the description and implementation of the individual research approaches. Furthermore, research results and their evaluations are also presented.

4.1 Customer survey as quantitative data collection method

The first research step is to identify which of the dimensions and factors listed above are most relevant to VW customers. This approach is intended to shorten the model to only relevant dimensions and factors in order to conduct a more focused research within the focus groups and individual interviews later. This is aimed at not to overexploit the participants' work motivation. This should strengthen the significance of the results.

The questionnaire is designed to identify which dimensions and factors are most important to VW customers.[1] The following list represents the conditions of participation:

1. The participants must either own or use a Volkswagen AG model of car.

2. The use or possession of a Volkswagen AG vehicle may not be more than three years ago.

3. The participants are not allowed to bring in their own opinion about the VW-DES. This level of data collection aims solely at determining how relevant the individual dimensions and factors are for VW customers.

4. The participants are only allowed to give the predefined options for responses.

---

[1] The entire questionnaire, including the survey matrix was developed collaboratively by the authors and the consulting firm 'Synergetic Management Consulting Group' (SMCG).

5. The participants must all have the same understanding of the background of the dimensions and factors so that results are not distorted.

The questionnaire is send out to over 200 VW customers affected by the VW-DES. As the only segmentation criterion is a personal affectedness a rather small group of respondents is needed to evaluate findings which is achieved by 50 valid responses (cf. Mossig 2012).

4.2   Focus groups as qualitative data collection method

The participants of the focus groups are contacted either by phone or in person. However, due the 'Covid-19' pandemic outbreak, social networks are also used as a recruitment platform, as personal contacts are very limited, by order of the government. Incentives such as free drinks or small snacks should motivate suitable individuals to participate in the focus groups. It makes sense to formulate specific questions that could help in the selection of participants, since participants have to fit into the desired pattern (cf. Morgan 1999). Two focus groups are conducted showing a very homogenous response structure and content. The following represents the five conditions of participation:

1. The participant must have owned or used a Volkswagen AG vehicle brand within the last three years.

2. The participant must be familiar with the DES from Volkswagen, but not in the most detailed form.

3. The participant must be willing to share his opinion about the Volkswagen DES with others.

4. The participant must be willing to implement constructive group discussions and joint elaborations.

5. The participant must adhere to the rules within the focus groups set by the moderator/researcher in advance (this contains also the actual 'Covid-19-rules' set by the government).

4.3   Individual customer interviews

To substantiate the statements of the focus group participants, individual interviews with twelve VW customers were conducted. This research method should result in the evaluation of the focus group participants' suggestions on how to close trust gaps according to personal importance. This was done via a ranking system. From this it could be deduced which measures were more strongly desired by customers than others. The results of the interviews were already taken into account in the presentation of results in chapter 4.6.

4.4   Presentation of survey results

During the evaluation of the quantitative research, a sum index is used. The sum index can result from simple addition as well as from averaging. With the simple addition, a so-called addition index, the individual values are added across the variables (cf. Hadler 2019).

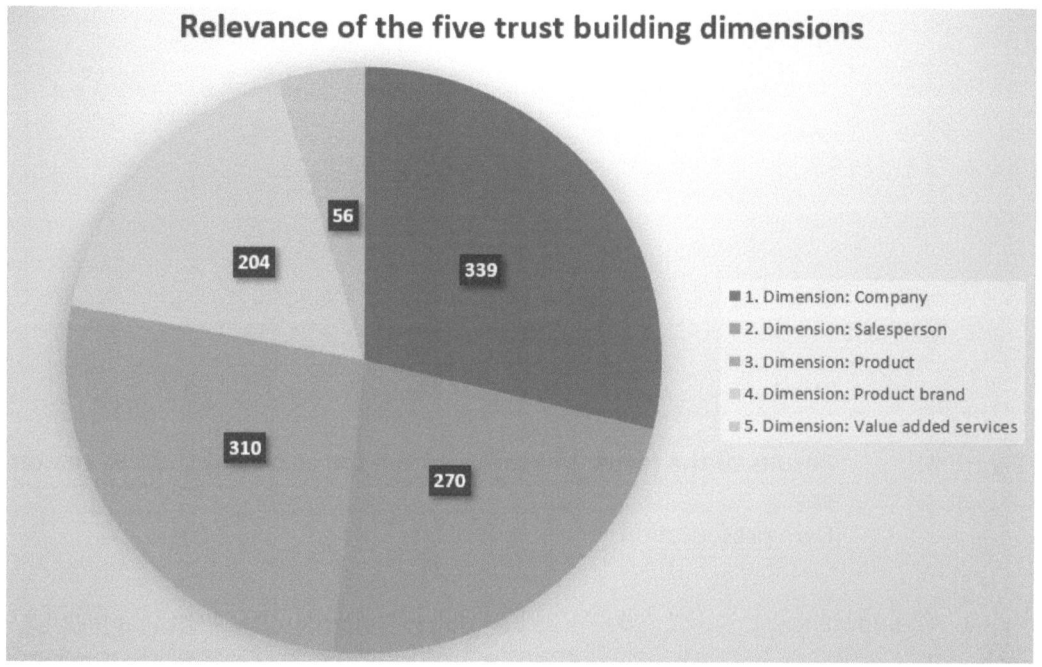

Figure 5:   **Results of the dimensional relevance within the survey of the VW customers**
Own presentation

1. Company   →   339 Points (The strongest relevance)

2. Salesperson   →   270 Points (The third strongest relevance)

3. Product   →   310 Points (The second strongest relevance)

Based on the results shown in Figure 5, it can be seen, that the respective trust-building dimensions are of varying relevance to VW customers. Therefore, **hypothesis H1a is to be confirmed.**

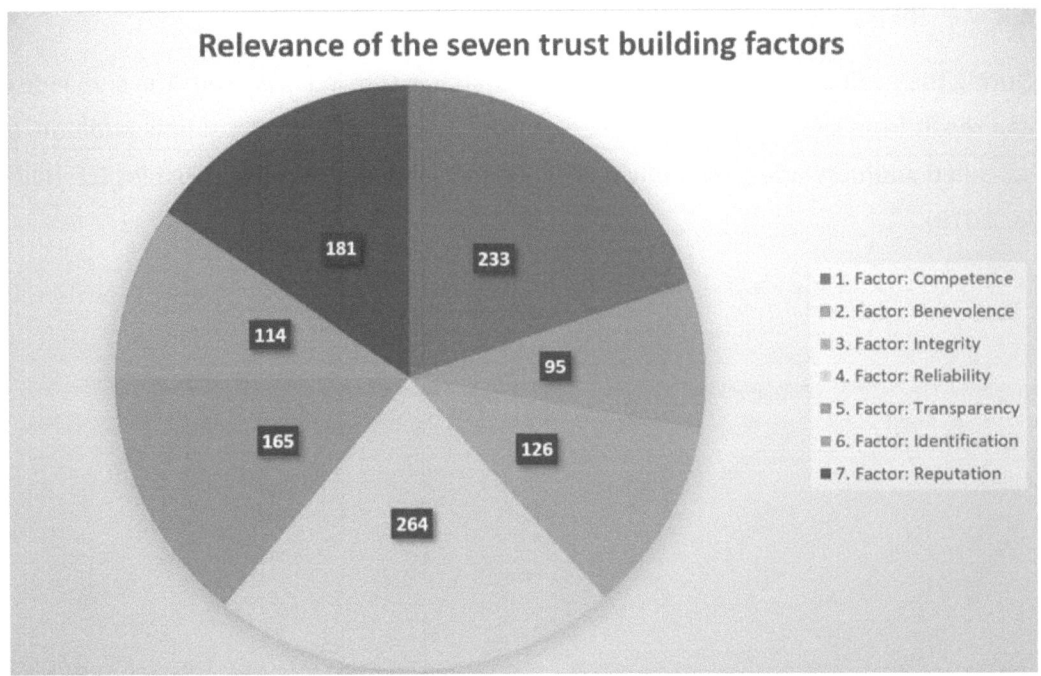

Figure 6:   **Results of the factor relevance within the survey of the VW customers**
Own presentation

1. Competence   →   233 Points (The second strongest relevance)

2. Reliability   →   264 Points (The strongest relevance)

3. Transparency   →   165 Points (The fourth strongest relevance)

4. Reputation   →   181 Points (The third strongest relevance

The trust-building factors shown in Figure 6 also reveal differences in terms of the relevance indicated by the customers. Thus, **hypothesis H1b is to be accepted**.

Hence it can be stated that respondents were clearly in a position to pinpoint the most relevant trust dimensions and trust factors when reflecting Volkswagen.

4.5   Review of the research hypotheses within the focus groups

A common procedure for analysing qualitative information is often applied "simultaneously with data collection, data interpretation, and narrative report writing" (Creswell 1994 after Davis/Smith 2005: 471). This report assists in supporting/refusing the hypotheses. In the course of this chapter, the remaining research hypotheses are monitored with regard to the results and findings within the focus groups.

The five trust building dimensions and the seven trust building factors

H2:	Particular constellations between trust-building dimensions and trust-building factors indicate trust gaps within the DES at VW for Customers.

Within the research with the focus groups, it became clear that the participants have predominantly negative associations with VW when they take the exhaust gas scandal into account. Apart from a few positive statements, the negative ones predominate. Therefore, it can be stated that the VW diesel scandal has shaken the trust of the customers with regard to the corresponding trust-building dimensions and factors. **Hypothesis H2 can therefore be confirmed.**

> H3:   Within the compositional framework of the trust-building dimensions and trust-building factors, VW customers are able to give precise reasons for the loss of trust in the Volkswagen AG.

In order to identify whether the focus group participants could give precise reasons that led to the loss of trust, it became apparent that the deterioration of trust was mainly addressed to the management of Volkswagen AG, as they according to the participants showed misconduct in several respects. In the discussion within the focus groups, it became obvious that the loss of trust could be explicitly explained by the participants with regard to the individual trust building dimensions and factors. **Therefore, hypothesis H3 is to be accepted.**

> H4:   Identified gaps in trust can be effectively closed via adapted measures that meet the expectations of VW customers.

The final task of the focus group participants was to explore possible measures that could close the previously identified trust gaps in terms of each of the trust-building dimensions and factors. Each participant was asked to put forward one measure for each possible combination. These measures were then evaluated by other VW customers using a scoring scale and then clustered into categories. The documentation of the results can be found in chapter 4.6. As different measures to close the trust gaps were identified, **hypothesis H4 can be verified.**

4.6   Presentation of the focus groups results

The results of the qualitative research are presented graphically. The possibilities for closing identified trust gaps are based on the statements of the focus group participants, as well as the statements of the VW customers interviewed. Therefore, final recommendations for action can be made regarding the individual trust-building dimensions and factors that can rebuild trust in the corresponding segments.

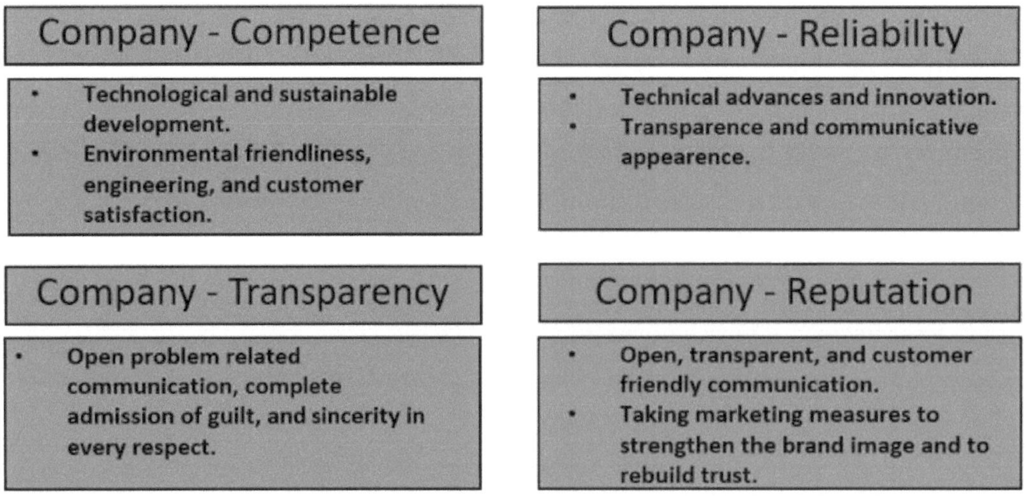

Company - Competence	Company - Reliability
• Technological and sustainable development. • Environmental friendliness, engineering, and customer satisfaction.	• Technical advances and innovation. • Transparence and communicative appearence.

Company - Transparency	Company - Reputation
• Open problem related communication, complete admission of guilt, and sincerity in every respect.	• Open, transparent, and customer friendly communication. • Taking marketing measures to strengthen the brand image and to rebuild trust.

Figure 7: **Final recommendations for action for dimension 'company'**
Own presentation

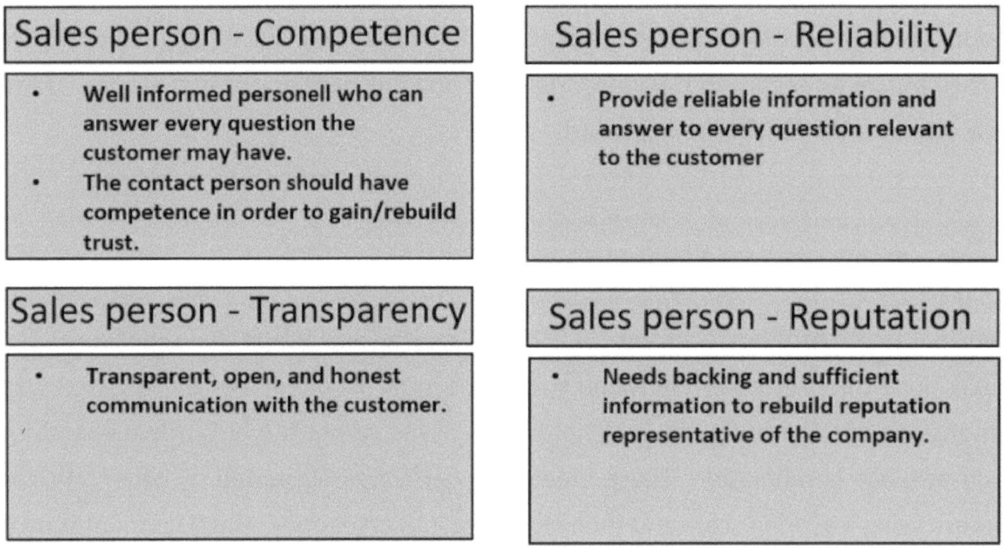

Sales person - Competence	Sales person - Reliability
• Well informed personell who can answer every question the customer may have. • The contact person should have competence in order to gain/rebuild trust.	• Provide reliable information and answer to every question relevant to the customer

Sales person - Transparency	Sales person - Reputation
• Transparent, open, and honest communication with the customer.	• Needs backing and sufficient information to rebuild reputation representative of the company.

Figure 8: **Final recommendations for action for the dimension 'sales person'**
Own presentation

Product - Competence	Product - Reliability
• True and correct details of all information and vehicle data provided. • Making technological advances for customer satisfaction and competetiveness.	• To be technologically advanced and facilitate innovation. • Pay attention to environmental friendliness when developing innovations and new technologies. • Only develop products where the product information is honest and reliable.

Product - Transparency	Product - Reputation
• Constant and honest communication with the public regarding product information and values, such as vehicle exhaust and consumption.	• Offering the customer good product quality.

Figure 9:   Final recommendations for action for dimension 'product'
Own presentation

Figure 7 to Figure 9 show that VW customers are able to define specific recommendations for improvement with which the lost trust can be restored. All participants are very clear about where trust deteriorated and how it can be restored. It is particularly clear that, above all, more honesty and openness is desired across all dimensions. By admitting omissions and mistakes made, it is possible to close the trust gaps that have arisen, with the suggestions from VW customers who participated. Furthermore, it can be seen proposed that the desired measures are primarily a matter of implementation by the authorised members of the group VW, i.e. the management. This mainly stirred the ire of customers and the general public. The results of the research show that lost customer trust can be restored with appropriate measures to customers and the public. A suitable communication policy on the part of VW would support all these measures. Nevertheless, internal company communication is also of crucial importance, as the employees, as representatives of the group, play a major role in the implementation of the measures

5   Conclusion

Findings appear to show that the modified trust model by Kreikenberg can be adapted to a more simplified model. The application of this new approach shows satisfactory results as regards a) identifying relevant trust dimensions and trust factors for a specific case, b) identifying the correlations between relevant dimensions and factors, c) identifying relevant gaps in trust concerning the case examined and finally d) triggering specific measures to close trust gaps identified. For the case under investigation i.e. Volkswagen and the DES it can be stated that measures identified to close existing trust gaps appear pragmatically applicable and make common sense. Hence there are indications that the adapted model for measuring trust and identifying subsequent measures to close trust gaps appears to work satisfactory.

References

Ahlström, C.; Gesper, T. (2007): Der Erfolg von Handelsmarken. Welche Strategien die Position der Marke stärken ; Ergebnisse einer umfangreichen Studie. Hamburg: Diplomica-Verl. (Diplomica).

Andresen, J.-E. (2019): Immer mehr Hersteller und Modelle vom Dieselskandal betroffen (https://www.myright.de/magazin/abgasskandal/immer-mehr-hersteller-und-modelle-vom-dieselskandal-betroffen). Accessed on 07.10.2020.

Bagdoniene, L.; Jakstaite, R. (2009): Trust as basis for development of relationships between professional service providers and their clients. In: Economics and Management, 14. (2009), pp. 360–366.

Balderjahn, I. (2010): Vertrauen schaffende Marken-Kommunikation [Vortrag]. Universität Potsdam. Berlin. (25.01.2010).

Berndt, R.; Fantapié Altobelli, C.; Sander, M. (2010): Internationales Marketing-Management. Berlin, Heidelberg: Springer Berlin Heidelberg.

Bratzel, S.; Verbraucherzentrale Bundesverband (ed.) (2018): Der Abgasskandal und die Vertrauenskrise im Automobilmarkt - Ursachen, Lösungen und Auswirkungen auf den Ver-braucher. Bergisch Gladbach.

Bruhn, M.; Straßer, M. (2014): Wertsteigerung durch Value Added Products in Dienstleis-tungsunternehmen. Konzept und empirische Befunde für einen verhaltensorientierten Service Value. In: Bruhn, M.; Hadwich, K. (eds.): Service Value als Werttreiber. Konzepte, Messung und Steuerung. Wiesbaden: Springer Gabler (Forum Dienstleistungsmanage-ment), pp. 301–328.

Colquitt, J.; Scott, B.; LePine, J. (2007): Trust, Trustworthiness, and Trust Propensity: A Meta-Analytic Test of Their Unique Relationships with Risk Taking and Job Performance. In: The Journal of applied psychology, 92. (2007), pp. 909–927.

Comer, J. M.; Plank, R. E.; Reid, D. A.; Pullins, E. B. (1999): Methods in Sales Research: Perceived Trust in Business-to-Business Sales: A New Measure. In: Journal of Personal Selling & Sales Management, 19. (1999), No. 3, pp. 61–71.

Davies, G.; Olmedo-Cifuentes, I. (2016): Corporate misconduct and the loss of trust. In: European Journal of Marketing, 50. (2016), No. 7/8, pp. 1426–1447.

Davis, S. F.; Smith, R. A. (2005): An introduction to statistics and research methods. Becoming a psychological detective. 1st ed., Upper Saddle River, NJ: Pearson/Prentice Hall.

Eckl-Dorna, W. (2015): Klagewelle gegen Volkswagen - Der Länder-Überblick (https://www.manager-magazin.de/unternehmen/autoindustrie/volkswagen-abgas-skandal-welche-staaten-klagen-bereits-gegen-vw-a-1055774.html). Accessed on 07.10.2020.

Ennew, C.; Sekhon, H. (2007): Measuring trust in financial services: the Trust Index. In: Consumer Policy Review, 17. (2007), pp. 62–68.

Fulmer, C. A.; Gelfand, M. J. (2012): At What Level (and in Whom) We Trust: Trust Across Multiple Organizational Levels. In: Journal of Management, 38. (2012), No. 4, pp. 1167–1230.

Gietl, J. (2016): Vertrauen lässt sich nicht einfordern. Interview. In: Shift. Das Nachhal-tig-keitsmagazin von Volkwagen 2016. Volkswagen AG (ed.).

Guenzi, P.; Johnson, M. D.; Castaldo, S. (2009): A comprehensive model of customer trust in two retail stores. In: Journal of Service Management, 20. (2009), No. 3, pp. 290–316.

Hadler, M. (2019): Quantitative Datenanalyse in den Sozialwissenschaften. Vom Fra-gebogen zu ersten Auswertungen. 2., überarbeitete Auflage,

Hatak, I. (2018): Kompetenz, Vertrauen und Kooperation. Eine experimentelle Studie. 1st, New ed., Frankfurt a.M : Peter Lang GmbH Internationaler Verlag der Wis-senschaften (For-schungsergebnisse der Wirtschaftsuniversität Wien, vol. 50).

Jänig, C. (2004): Wissensmanagement. Die Antwort auf die Herausforderungen der Globa-lisierung. Berlin, Heidelberg, s.l. : Springer Berlin Heidelberg.

Kreikenberg, A. H. (2013): A Framework of Customer Trust Measurement. [phd]; Uni-versity of Glocuestershire (ed.), Glasgow/Dortmund.

Leonidou, L. C.; Kvasova, O.; Leonidou, C. N.; Chari, S. (2013): Business Unethicality as an Impediment to Consumer Trust: The Moderating Role of Demographic and Cultural Charac-teristics. In: Journal of Business Ethics, 112. (2013), No. 3, pp. 397–415.

Lewis, J. D. (2007): Trusted partners, how companies build mutual trust and win to-gether. [Place of publication not identified] : Free Press.

Lorbeer, A. (2003): Vertrauensbildung in Kundenbeziehungen. Ansatzpunkte zum Kun-den-bindungsmanagement. Wiesbaden: Deutscher Universitätsverlag (Schrif-tenreihe der Handelshochschule Leipzig).

Martín, S. S.; Camarero, C. (2005): Consumer Reactions to Firm Signals in Asymmetric Relationships. In: Journal of Service Research, 8. (2005), No. 1, pp. 79–97.

Mayer, R. C.; Davis, J. H.; Schoorman, F. D. (1995): An Integrative Model of Organiza-tional Trust. In: The Academy of Management Review, 20. (1995), No. 3, p. 709.

Menzel, S. (2019): Bei VW herrscht noch immer großer Vertrauensverlust. Der Auto-konzern leidet noch immer unter den Folgen der Dieselaffäre. Um Vertrauen zurückzugewinnen, setzt VW verstärkt auf Elektromobilität. (https://www.handelsblatt.com/unternehmen/industrie/volkswagen-bei-vw-herrscht-noch-immer-grosser-vertrauensverlust-/24467858.html). Accessed on 07.10.2020.

Mohr, J.; Nevin, J. R. (1990): Communication Strategies in Marketing Channels: A The-oreti-cal Perspective. In: Journal of Marketing, 54. (1990), No. 4, p. 36.

Morgan, D. L. (1999): The focus group guidebook. [Nachdr.], Thousand Oaks: SAGE (Fo-cus group kit, vol. 1).

Mossig, I. (2012): Stichproben, Stichprobenauswahlverfahren und Berechnung des minimal erforderlichen Stichprobenumfangs. Bremen (vol. 1) (http://hdl.handle.net/10419/90425). Accessed on 29.05.2021.

Netflix (2018): Tödliches NOx. (Dirty Money) (https://www.netflix.com/watch/80149533?trackId=13752289&tctx=0%2C0%2C9cc412f88815cb96c18aaa9cbdeb5dce4eccc842%3Ac9b74b187c8b3d4ff846d67c3470e7a0ab80c3ac%2C%2C). Accessed on 07.10.2020.

Neumaier, M. (2010): Vertrauen im Entscheidungsprozess. Der Einfluss unbewusster Prozesse im Konsumentenverhalten. Wiesbaden: Gabler Verlag / Springer Fach-medien Wiesbaden GmbH Wiesbaden (Forschungsgruppe Konsum und Verhalten).

Peters, M. (2008): Vertrauen in Wertschöpfungspartnerschaften zum Transfer von re-tenti-vem Wissen. Wiesbaden: Springer Fachmedien (Information - Organisation - Produktion).

Pirson, M. (2007): Facing the Trust Gap. Meaning and Building Trust in Organizations. [Dissertation]; University of St. Gallen (ed.), St. Gallen.

Richter, K. (2016): Abgestiegen und ausgelistet - Volkswagwen fällt tief. In: Shift. Das Nachhaltigkeitsmagazin von Volkwagen 2016. Volkswagen AG (ed.), pp. 18–19.

Rossmann, A. (2010): Vertrauen in Kundenbeziehungen. Wiesbaden: Gabler Verlag / Springer Fachmedien Wiesbaden GmbH Wiesbaden (Marketing-Management).

Schmidt, H. (2016): Der Abgaskrieg. Am Limit. 2. Auflage, Norderstedt: Books on Demand.

Schoorman, F. D.; Mayer, R. C.; Davis, J. H. (2007): An Integrative Model of Organizational Trust: Past, Present, and Future. In: The Academy of Management Review, 32. (2007), No. 2, pp. 344–354.

Shockley-Zalabak, P. S.; Morreale, S. P. (2011): Building high-trust organizations. In: Lea-der to Leader, 2011. (2011), No. 60, pp. 39–45.

Statista (2016): Meinung zu VW nach dem Diesel Skandal in Deutschland 2016 (https://de.statista.com/statistik/daten/studie/631507/umfrage/meinung-zu-volkswagen-nach-dem-dieselskandal/). Accessed on 07.10.2020.

Statista (2020): Umfrage zum Vertrauen in deutsche Automarken in Deutschland 2020 (https://de.statista.com/statistik/daten/studie/1100094/umfrage/umfrage-zum-vertrauen-in-deutsche-automarken-in-deutschland/). Accessed on 07.10.2020.

Volkswagen AG; Volkswagen AG (ed.) (2016): Shift. Das Nachhaltigkeitsmagazin von Volkswagen 2016.

Wünschmann, S.; Müller, S. (2006): Markenvertrauen. Ein Erfolgsfaktor des Marken-mana-gements. In: Bauer, H. H. (ed.): Konsumentenvertrauen. Konzepte und Anwendungen für ein nachhaltiges Kundenbindungsmanagement. München: Vahlen, pp. 221–234.

The Authors

Prof. Dr. Ralf A. Brickau obtained a double degree at the University of Applied Sciences in Dortmund and the University of Plymouth after studying business administration. In 1993 he completed his doctorate at the University of Plymouth and at the same time received a Diploma in Marketing from the Chartered Institute of

Marketing. He then worked as a key account manager for a trading and service agency in the food industry. In 1998, Brickau was appointed professor at FHW Berlin before joining FH Dortmund and ISM in 2001. In the last 15 years he has worked as a consultant for numerous companies, including Volkswagen, Fujitsu, BVB 09, Lambertz, BMW, Mercedes-Benz, Signal Iduna, REWE, Ferrero, Frosta and Apetito. Analysis, planning and strategy play an important role not only in his job but also in his free time: he regularly takes part in sailing regattas. His main research interests are strategy development, brand building, trust management, neuroscientific aspects of POS marketing and CRM/sales management in different industries.

Prof. Dr. Christoph Moss teaches communication and marketing at the International School of Management. He is considered an expert in newsroom organisation and has implemented more than 100 corporate newsrooms – for example at Siemens, Fraport or Swiss Life Germany. In addition to stations at other

universities, Christoph Moss worked at Deutsche Bank as well as at broadcasters and newspapers in Düsseldorf, Passau, Dresden, Dortmund, Brussels and Paris. He was managing editor in the Handelsblatt newsroom and headed the Georg von Holtzbrinck School for Business Journalists.

Simon Stotz studied Strategic Marketing Management and Management in the Master's programme (M. A and M. Sc.) at the International School of Management Dortmund and at Napier University Edinburgh in Scotland. Before, during and after his studies, Mr Stotz was passionate about customer trust, sales psychology, strategy development and consulting. During an internship at Deutsche Tel-

ekom in innovation management, he was able to expand his technical knowledge and learn about the customer requirements of tomorrow. Together with Prof. Dr. Ralf A. Brickau, he works on various projects, such as supervising a comprehensive consulting project of ISM Master students, in order to pass on his acquired knowledge to the next generations. In his professional future, Stotz will continue to deal with the topics of customer trust, consumer behaviour and sales psychology.

Daniel Meierhof studied information technology at the TU Dortmund from 2001 to 2005 and also completed a degree in com-
puter science at the IT Center Dortmund in 2008. During his dual
studies he developed CRM and ERP systems and dealt with marketing issues at the same time. As a result, he was appointed to
the university and has been responsible for marketing and communication at the ITC since 2008. Together with Prof. Dr. Brickau

he has looked after customers as a partner at SMCG since 2010 and lectured at the same
time at the ISM and the ITC. He is particularly interested in BI and neuromarketing topics. But also projects for value chain optimization, customer expectation management
and branding for customers in the automotive, food and energy supply industries are
part of his knowledge. In his private life he likes to sail with his family and goes boulder-
ing and climbing as a compensation for his job. Since 2021, Meierhof has been an IT
project manager at a software company and at the same time a freelancer for strategic
development in the university environment.

Stotz, Simon; Brickau, Ralf A.; Moss, Christoph; Meierhof, Daniel:
Measuring and Restoring customer trust - an explorative research based on the VW Diesel
gate scandal

International School of Management

Die International School of Management (ISM) – eine staatlich anerkannte, private Hochschule – bildet seit 1990 in Dortmund, Frankfurt/Main, München, Hamburg, Köln, Stuttgart und Berlin Nachwuchsführungskräfte für die internationale Wirtschaft aus. Das Studienprogramm umfasst sieben Vollzeit-Bachelor-Studiengänge, neun Vollzeit-Master-Studiengänge, einen fachfremden Master-Studiengang, einen vorbereitenden Pre-Master sowie drei duale Studiengänge und drei berufsbegleitende Programme (B.A. Business Administration, M.A. Management, MBA General Management). Alle Studiengänge der ISM zeichnen sich durch ihre Internationalität und Praxisorientierung aus. Diese Erfolgsfaktoren garantiert die ISM durch enge Kooperationen mit Unternehmen, Projekte in Kleingruppen sowie integrierte Auslandssemester und -module an weltweit über 175 Partnerhochschulen. Die Qualität der Ausbildung bestätigen Studierende und Ehemalige ebenso wie Personaler in zahlreichen Hochschulrankings. Die ISM belegt dort seit Jahren konstant vorderste Plätze.

Mit dem ISM Working Paper werden Ergebnisse von Arbeiten präsentiert, wie z. B. Thesen, Ergebnisse aus Workshops oder aus eigenen Forschungsarbeiten. Ähnlich wie beim ISM Research Journal, das ebenfalls zu den neuen ISM Publikationsreihen gehört, werden die Beiträge im ISM Working Paper einem fachlichen Bewertungsverfahren (Peer Review) unterzogen.

Previously published issues in the series „ISM Workingpaper":

No. 1	Brock, S.; Antretter, T.: Kapitalkostenermittlung als Grauzone wertorientierter Unternehmensführung, 2014
No. 2	Ohlwein, M.: Die Prüfung der globalen Güte eines Kausalmodells auf Stabilität mit Hilfe eines nichtparametrischen Bootstrap-Algorithmus, 2015
No. 3	Lütke Entrup, M.; Simmert, D. B.; Tegethoff, C.: Die Entwicklung des Working Capital in Private Equity Portfoliounternehmen, 2017
No. 4	Ohlwein, M.: Kultur- vs. regionenbezogene Abgrenzung von Ländergruppen. Eine clusteranalytische Untersuchung auf Basis der Kulturdimensionen nach Hofstede, 2017
No. 5	Lütke Entrup, M.; Simmert, D. B.; Caspari, L.: Die Performance von deutschen Portfoliounternehmen nach Private Equity Buyouts, 2017
No. 6	Brickau, R. A.; Cornelsen, J.: The impact of visual subliminal triggers at the point of sale on the consumers' willingsness to purchase – A critical investigation into gender differences, 2017
No. 7	Hampe, L.; Rommel, K.: Einflüsse von kognitiven Verzerrungen auf das Anlageverhalten deutscher Privataktionäre, 2017
No. 8	Brickau, R. A.; Röhricht, J.: Archaische Gesten im POS-Marketing – Die Nutzung archaischer Gesten in der Display- und Plakatwerbung, 2017
No. 9	Fontanari, M.; Kredinger, D.: Risiko- und Resilienzbewusstsein. Empirische Analysen und erste konzeptionelle Ansätze zur Steigerung der Resilienzfähigkeit von Regionen, 2017
No. 10	Schröder, C.; Weber, U.: Integration von Flüchtlingen in den Arbeitsmarkt als Chance für Diversity Management: Einführung und ausgewählte Beispiele im Kreis Steinfurt, 2017
No. 11	Zimmermann, N. A.; Gericke, J.: Supply Chain Risiko-management – Analyse des Status Quo und neuer Entwicklungstendenzen, 2018

Stotz, Simon; Brickau, Ralf A.; Moss, Christoph; Meierhof, Daniel:
Measuring and Restoring customer trust - an explorative research based on the VW Diesel gate scandal

No. 12	Haberstock, P.; Weber, G.; Jägering, C.: Process of Digital Transformation in Medium-Sized Enterprises - an Applied Re-search Study, 2018
No. 13	Potaszkin, I.; Weber, U.; Groffmann, N.: „Die süße Alternative" Smart Health: Akzeptanz der Telemedizin bei Diabetikern, 2018
No. 14	Holthaus, L.; Horn, C.; Perret, J. K.: E-Commerce im Luxusmarkensegment – Die Sicht deutscher Kundinnen am Beispiel Chanel, 2020
No. 15	Bingemer, S.; Ohlwein, M.: Mit Customer Experience Management die Digitalisierung meistern – Die Rolle von Unternehmenskultur und -organisation, 2020
No. 16	Gildemeister, C. C.; Mehn, A.; Perret, J. K.: Factory-Outlet-Center: Discount oder Disney?, 2021
No. 17	Böge, Carlotta; Perret, Jens K.; Netzel, Janine: Die Effekte der Zielorientierung auf den Berufserfolg – Erste empirische Befunde, 2021
No. 18	Stotz, Simon; Brickau, Ralf A.; Moss, Christoph, Meierhof, Daniel: Measuring and Restoring customer trust - an explorative research based on the VW Diesel gate scandal, 2021